274·9415

WHY

THE IRISH CHURCH

DESERVES TO DIE

First published in 2017 by

columba press

23 Merrion Square

Dublin 2, Ireland

www.columba.ie

ISBN: 978 1 78218 339 6

Set in Linux Libertine 12/16
Cover and book design by Alba Esteban | Columba Press
Printed by ScandBook, Sweden

WHY

THE IRISH CHURCH

DESERVES TO DIE

Joe McDonald

columba press

†

About the Author

Father Joe McDonald is the eldest of four children born to Bridie and Joe McDonald. He was born in West Belfast in 1961 and spent many years as a Christian Brother, serving a number of roles in teaching, management and giving school retreats. He was the last brother headmaster in the Abbey Christian Brothers Grammar School, Newry and has taught English, Psychology and Religious Studies.

Father McDonald holds degrees in Theology, Education and Educational Management. Ten years ago he was ordained a priest for the Archdiocese of Dublin, and has been parish priest of St Matthew's, Ballyfermot, Dublin for five years. He has previously served as a pastor in St Michael's, Athy, and Our Lady of Good Counsel, Johnstown, Killiney.

Father McDonald writes a popular weekly column in the parish newsletter entitled, 'Rumblings from the Bunker'. Over the past few years he has been a regular guest on *The Late Debate*, *Vincent Browne* and *Claire Byrne Live*.

His interests include dogs, travel, genealogy, reading and music.

Contents

† FOREWORD

You will learn many things from this thought provoking book. Father Joe McDonald likes incense, the fragrant aroma we encounter wafting though the church at the end of a funeral - or 'holy smoke' as one of his parishioners called it.

But this book will incense many – but Joe knows this – he asks more questions than answers but it is a challenging, learned, humourous and noble endeavour.

But while Father Joe has no fear of incensing debate – he does not take offence easily – something the Irish church could take on board.

Administering communion recently he admits that only a small percentage said 'amen' on receiving the host – the majority retorted with 'cheers', 'nice one' and 'sound job'. While one of his confreres took offence at this, Joe was grateful that so many had celebrated the Eucharist.

Nor did he send for the doctrinal police when, upon returning from a break, he was told by a member of his congregation that the "parish sister said a few great Masses when you were away", this was not met by umbrage but by Joe's hearty laugh.

But make no mistake this elegantly written tome will challenge many – including those in authority within the church.

Joe argues that the church is far too defensive when it comes to national debate, believing as he does that controversial issues are often met with denial and complacency.

It is a clarion call to the church to get involved in national discourse, while lamenting on how some clerics were let down by the silence of the Bishops. He simply believes that the church is much too quiet.

I know the church or anyone else has no obligation to participate in the public square of national discourse, but in a country where it is not beneath the chief executive of the largest airline in the world to ring a phone show – can we ever imagine an Irish bishop being so proactive?

It is fifty-one years since the infamous "bishop and the Nightie affair" when the irate Bishop of Clonfert proactively attacked an innocuous quiz item on the Late Late show, subjecting himself to national ridicule. It is surely time to forget that episode from 1966 and call on the church leadership to have no fear of entering national discussion.

These are just some of the issues raised in this important, timely and provocative book.

It should be read in the spirit in which it is written – though I can see how some of those in the church leadership might be upset by it, but Joe is not the enemy. It is denial and complacency that deserves that moniker.

I know it is hard to hear one of their most high profile priests say 'the church in Ireland is dying, the signs of hope are few' – but Joe has no fear of inconvenient truths.

But it deserves to be read by people outside the church. There are many in Ireland who now profess that 'I've no faith but I like my priest.'

I guarantee that not only will they find this book very entertaining - after all Neil Young, Leonard Cohen, Jimmy McCarthy and Patrick Kavanagh get pride of place beside the Gospels of Matthew, Mark, Luke and John, the ideas and issues raised will linger for a long time.

Equally I was reminded reading this book of Joe, of the quote from John Lennon, 'Life is what happens when you are busy making plans' – or as he says 'in the mess than can be life'.

Neither does he lapse into defensive mode, never dismissing those who are critical as 'having an anti church agenda'. While the clarion call is for more of the laity to be directly involved in the running of the church – Joe knows that resistance might come from some of the laity.

Through my mother, Mabel's, attendance at Joe's weekly Mass in St Matthews church I always get his Sunday newsletters including his column *Rumblings from the Bunker* – some of which are included in the appendix. In this weekly missive he takes on difficult subjects, and on first reading one might miss some of the nuances in his thoughtful and engaging writings. That's why this book deserves more than a cursory reading.

One constant theme running through his writings – often witty and self deprecating – is his weekly acknowledgment of those hurt by the church to accept his embrace and that of Christ if they wish to return.

There are many new ideas in these pages – not least of all his revolutionary idea for a new community embracing the laity and clergy.

As the Irish church prepares for the world meeting of families and the imminent visit of Pope Frances to Dublin this book could not be more timely. This is a brave, thoughtful and serious call for a national debate – deeply embedded in Father Joe McDonald's faith and his ultimate belief in the hope that is Jesus Christ.

Joe Duffy.
Broadcaster and author.
August 2017

INTRODUCTION

The present death of the Irish church provides the faith community with a unique opportunity. This is a time when we can unite ourselves in a most profound way with the suffering Messiah. The Irish church knows Gethsemane and in some significant ways and knows Calvary also. As well as being united with the passion, we are also afforded in these days an opportunity to bear witness to the paschal mystery unfolding around us. This invitation to face what is dying in the daily reality of church is not an invitation to gloom. In fact in turning to face this death we exhibit spiritual health, courage and most importantly, a living faith. If we fail to do so then we cannot even begin to become Easter people. While it is true that the future of the church is in God's hands, if this concept that is taken to the extreme, it can lead to a real laziness among Catholics.

What qualifies me to speak about the church at this time? I have been blessed with a strong Catholic faith from childhood. At the same time, I have personal experience of clerical abuse and its cover up. I am painfully aware of the fragility, brokenness and continued capacity of the church to be abusive. In all this, it remains the church that I love. The church is my passion.

As I write, for the first time in over one hundred and fifty years, the Archdiocese of Dublin has no entrant to the seminary, though we are blessed with two ordinations to the priesthood later in the year. By 2020 there will be less than two hundred priests working in a diocese of over one million Catholics. The number of priests in the diocese is expected to fall. Many of the priests are elderly and there is a growing incidence of a wide range of health issues among them. They continue to serve over two hundred parishes.

In conjunction with this scenario it is interesting to note the huge majority yes vote in the recent same-sex marriage referendum, the imminent campaign to repeal the eighth amendment, and the upcoming debate regarding end of life issues. Now let us place these in the context of the one million Catholics in this diocese, the vast majority of whom have completed fourteen years in Catholic education. Recently I heard some senior figures in the church take comfort from information gleaned in the recent census. (78.3 per cent of the population identifies itself as Catholic, which is a significant decline from 84.2 per cent in 2011.) I take little comfort from these statistics. To me they asked the wrong question. What people acknowledged was their ethnic origin and background; of course for a high percentage of people that is Roman Catholic. I wonder: if the question had been framed around weekly or monthly attendance at Mass, what would the figures look like? If the church were a multinational, which of course it's not, there would be talk of crisis and emergency. Is there a crisis in the Irish church? Or is it worse? Are we witnessing the end of the Irish church? Should we be preparing the wake? Or is it timely to re-examine and refocus on the end goal, of the Irish church? Is it in fact less about preparing the wake and more about turning, in a very real way, to the process of awakening?

This short book challenges us to face up to the reality of a seriously ailing church. It is an attempt to give us as a church the 'reality check' that the Archbishop of Dublin, Diarmuid Martin spoke of in the immediate aftermath of the same-sex marriage referendum. The Papal Nuncio, Archbishop Charles Brown, just before he left us, warned that the church was at the edge of an actuarial cliff and about to go into free fall with regard to the number of priests in the country. All of this together reveals the signs of death. However the question is, how bad is it? And what can be done, if anything? Is the church a candidate for intensive care, or should we bring it to the morgue?

This book also exposes the delicate flower of hope. It is so delicate that there is no certainty that it will bloom. This book asks why we find ourselves in this position, reaches clear conclusions and makes suggestions for future development, what might constitute residual signs of life. This is an Easter book. It lives in the moment when there is the first crack of light in the darkness. It is the earliest moment of light on Easter morning. Not only does it not ignore the horror of Good Friday, it highlights it, precisely because it is a lived experience in the Irish church. But also because it reminds us that without living through Good Friday there will be no resurrection.

This book is aimed at those who have given up on the church, either the formally resigned, or the long-term adrift. It includes those who are becoming increasingly disillusioned with the church but who may still retain some affection for it. It is hoped that it will also contribute to the ongoing debate around the reform and renewal of the church. Whether addressing the present malaise or fanning glimmers of hope, this book is rooted in compassion.

I propose urgent intervention, in the form of prophetic leadership, as a possible way to new life. It is my view that a prophetic leadership, co-operating with God's grace, can make it possible for a new entity of church to be born. I suggest that this prophetic leadership would involve:

1. saying no, as in an active rejection of the abusive church of yesterday

2. saying a renewed yes to Jesus in a unique and personal way,

3. committing oneself to act as an envoy of church reform and renewal.

As a diocesan priest in the Irish church in 2017, I believe that the Holy Spirit is shaping me, by which I mean nudging, burning, breathing and baptising me into the roles of monk, undertaker, prophet and midwife to the church.

ONE

ECCLESIAL RUST

Then I was given a long cane as a measuring rod, and I was told, 'Go and measure God's sanctuary, and the altar, and the people who worship there; but leave out the outer court and do not measure it, because it has been handed over to pagans

– Revelation 11:1-3

> The king is gone
> But he's not forgotten
> This is the story
> Of a Johnny Rotten
> It's better to burn out
> Than it is to rust
> The king is gone
> But he's not forgotten.
>
> – Neil Young, 'My My, Hey Hey (Out of the Blue)'

The new famine

Depending on how we look at things, we can say that we live in exciting times or scary times. Perhaps we could tentatively agree on the words of the Bob Dylan song, 'the times they are a changing'. Recently, in preparation for a talk I was to give, I gathered material from recent speeches by Nigel Farage, Boris Johnston, and Donald Trump and compared them to speeches by Stalin, Mussolini and Hitler. I was shocked at the similarities. They all used fear to mobilize people. Recently it has been interesting to hear people, in both post-Brexit and post-election USA, speak about how fear influenced their vote. It is true that fear will often paralyse or de-energize you. More skillfully, or perhaps more manipulatively, used fear will shut us down, entrap us, enslave us. There is a lot of fear in the world today. There is a lot of fear in Ireland today. There is fear of illness and how our health system will respond. As I write I am listening to the story of a one-hundred-and-three-year-old woman who spent fifteen hours on a hospital trolley here in Dublin. There is fear of unemployment, fear of rent increase and ensuing homelessness, fear of the stranger, fear of not having enough. The opposite of fear is freedom.

Where is the church amidst this fog of fear? How effective is our preaching of the gospel against the darkening political landscape in Europe and further afield? Do we witness to gospel freedom? Recently a lady said to me that she imagined that it is a very difficult time to be a priest. Now, while I understand what she meant and agree that priesthood is certainly not without challenges, it strikes me that it is in fact a very exciting time to be a priest.

I love being a priest. Though I came to priesthood quite late, I give God daily thanks for my vocation. It is good to be a priest living on this small little island on the edge of Europe at a time of great spiritual darkness. This spiritual darkness is evident on an almost daily basis. Again and again people come to me (particularly males and between the ages of twenty-five and thirty-five) and repeatedly use the word empty. 'Father, I feel empty.' What is quite startling is that this word is often used by those who have a job, are in a relationship and initially appear to have very little to worry them. The reality is quite different. The reality is they are hungry. Very hungry.

They have chased the rainbows and gone down the cul-de-sacs and still they struggle with that inner vacuum. They, like countless others before them, fail to see that the answer to their ache, that their nourishment, their fulfillment and their hope is to be found in Jesus. They cannot be blamed for this. The odds are stacked against them. The natural spiritual tendency is harmed by aspects of the particular malaise within the Irish church. The often understandable rejection of the institutional church, and the justifiable critique of it, fuse together to lead not only to a dismissal of the church but also a dismissal of the gospel and indeed Jesus himself. We are witnessing a new famine, a new great hunger. It is no coincidence that the epitaph for the Irish church is sitting beside stories of increased addiction and rising suicide rates. Sadly, despite our claims to modern democracy, we continue to fail people with mental issues. The new famine is real.

However, this famine is not about potatoes. It is about an ailing spirit, it is about soul food. Thankfully we are not losing lives, but sadly we are losing souls. There is in fact another famine-like haemorrhage taking place. It is an ebbing away of our spiritual identity. Whether we accept it or not, we are now in a post-Christian era. Ireland is now one of the toughest mission fields in the world. Today those seeking to faithfully proclaim the gospel will not experience the harsh conditions of physical poverty that many of our missionary sisters and brothers of years past endured. However, we will wrestle with sustained opposition, loneliness, isolation and the ever-gnawing question regarding not only our effectiveness, but also our relevance.

Rust never sleeps

Rust Never Sleeps is an album by Canadian singer-songwriter Neil Young and American band Crazy Horse. It was released on 2 July 1979 by Reprise Records. Young used the phrase 'rust never sleeps' as a concept for his tour and a metaphor for artistic vitality. In other words, by staying the same, one is vulnerable to the corrosive effects of ageing and obsolescence.

People are still emigrating for work or a better lifestyle. But there is another mass emigration well under way.

This is the emigration from organized religion to secular humanism. It is against this backdrop that people often argue that you do not have to be religious to be a good person. This is true. Some go further than this, claiming they are Catholics, indeed good Catholics, but they do not go to Mass. Is this true? Can it be true? What does it mean to be Catholic in contemporary Ireland?

The purpose in this chapter is to face up to the reality of the Irish church today. This requires honesty and courage. The great danger is to slip into something that can so sadly be part of church life, that is, to indulge in tut-tutting and finger pointing. This is not only divisive but also unchristian. Another danger is relativism, which has at its heart the twin dangers of diluting the sacred and believing that such dilution does not matter or might even be desirable. This chapter seeks to identify the death throes of the Irish church. For many this will be difficult reading and indeed some may see it as an act of betrayal. I see it as a labour of love.

In front of the dying church, the easiest thing in the world would be to glibly say that this is the death before a resurrection. This is even the expected response and yet in my view it is one to be resisted. It is to be resisted because it is trite and simplistic and we have no guarantee that it is true. There may be a rebirth in the Irish church but it is certainly not a foregone conclusion. Defining church as a faith community belonging to the undying Universal Church may well be a reasonable argument. However local, and sometimes national churches do actually decline and die. Religious orders, parishes and faith communities die. The fact that we have not got around to burying some of them does not mean that they are not dead. Some will see this as a denial of the great virtue of hope. However, to adopt the default position that the Irish church will survive is to assume that survival is automatic and to consign our faith to the realm of Harry Potter. For us as a faith community to acknowledge that we are not bound to some auto-resurrection, that we are in death mode, is neither treacherous nor hopeless but is, I contend, both faithful and prophetic.

My outlook is that of an insider, albeit a disgruntled one. I bring a spiritual narkyness to this. I bring anger to the task at hand. Some of it is raw, not unbridled, but raw. It was worse before some personal work and healing. Forgiveness, on-going forgiveness for individuals and systems remains imperative. My anger is now in reasonable shape, though needs periodic attention. It can now be confidently called a spiritual anger. It was always spiritual because of God's grace working through parents, family, some good teachers and some good priests. It is even more spiritual now, again because of God's grace and now also because of ministry. As a wounded priest, I am something of a leaking bucket.

This will disappoint some and turn others off. I can understand this. It is nice to think that our leaders have it sussed. Actually, I believe that woundedness in the pastor can be a good thing, provided of course that he knows that he is wounded. He needs to be able to name the wound and be actively involved in a process of healing. This more than hints at spiritual direction and psychotherapy. The spiritual anger that I am speaking of is aimed at the church, not so much for the sins of the past, but the sins of today. We tend to think of the sins of the past as located in the realm of child sexual abuse and we agree that this was horrific. The toxic leak of this has seeped into every crevice of the church and will take a long time before the deep healing that is necessary will take place.

A source of deep concern and righteous anger is the continued presence of key factors that, at least in part, fed the past abuse and certainly enabled its secret continuation. Apart from the sad, sick individuals at the centre of the scandals, we now know that the horror was greatly exacerbated by clericalism, general abuse of power and a distorted sense of the church. So the spiritual anger I speak of may well be rooted in the past but it would not continue without the oxygen of today's ecclesial ills. Sadly, clericalism is alive and well as is the abuse of power. As priests we remain unique in our lack of accountability. Even on a simple level of our weekly sermon, we can trot out the most boring drivel more or less with impunity. In conversation people often remark on the inaudible, incoherent and weak content of the sermon. This is sometimes related to a lack of preparation. The worst perpetrator of bad preaching is the pastor who has given up on reading. All of our reading as priests does not have to be about Jesus or the Scriptures. But is it not a little strange if none of it is? Sometimes out of kindness people will make excuses for their priest: he is old, he works too hard, he means well, he is a very nice man. The reality is that the standard of preaching leaves a lot to be desired. It is true we have an ageing, tired priesthood. At the same time, some of the best sermons I have heard, and heard of, in the past few months have come from a priest of eighty years of age, whose sermons clearly emanate from his own deep prayerfulness and tangible, vibrant faith. There are many priests who prepare and do their best in terms of delivery. Some have a gift for preaching. This does not change the fact that many people go to Mass and dread or tolerate a sermon that could, indeed should, be much better in its preparation, content and delivery. The important question is: if a priest's sermon were poor would he know? The unregulated, unaccountable priesthood costs us dearly. Many people still massage our ego. Perhaps part of celibacy emphasises our need to have our egos stroked.

The fact remains that ours is still very much a hierarchical church and unless we say or do something quite off the wall, then the men up the line are unlikely to hear about it, or if they do, they are unlikely to do anything about it. Of course there is another reason why we are unlikely to do anything out of the established norm. This brings us to one of the great ills of the church, namely clericalism. While clericalism is wider than the problem of career-clerics, it certainly includes them. I refer to the men up the line because of course they are still men; there are no women up the line. More's the pity. We are the poorer for this. Are we seriously suggesting that if women were in key positions, I mean positions with real bite, that the church would not be very different? We deprive ourselves, most especially within the realms of leadership, of all the strength, beauty and extraordinary giftedness of the feminine. This represents one of the areas of reform and renewal that we continue to drag our heels on. But for our purposes here, back to clericalism. If you want to find it alive and well, go to the parish pastoral council that cannot meet, pray, never mind make decisions, without 'Father'. Some priests know and will periodically use the language of collaboration. However, just beneath this attractive veneer there lurks a different reality best summarised as 'Father's way or no way!' Clericalism is also very much alive in how some, and I stress some, more seasoned clergy treat the newly ordained. I have heard a few, though still too many, anecdotes of young and not-so-young priests who have been treated disrespectfully by their parish priest. I mean treated as glorified altar boys and constantly reminded how much they have to learn. At times this includes public censure or at least being slighted in the presence of others. Sadly, such behaviour is justified by claims that this is everyone's experience starting out. Serious thought should be given to the parish priest who will be the newly ordained's first experience of parish leadership.

Sometimes within diocesan priesthood we let ourselves down. Even today some priests can be very patronising and disrespectful towards religious sisters, viewing them as subservient or an adjunct to the clerical or ordained ministry. Glorified maids. Perhaps one of the worst examples of the ignorance of diocesan clergy that I have experienced is towards the religious brother. I am taken back to many years ago. I am sitting at the table in the monastery. There are another fourteen brothers at the table and the young curate who has just celebrated morning Mass for us has now joined us for breakfast He is a pleasant young man, ordained three years, enthusiastic and committed. As in any community, there was quite a collection of characters around the table, mostly middle aged, some older, two of us (myself included) under thirty. We were for the most part committed religious, a few particularly bright or gifted, many deeply spiritual, and one or possibly two saints. On this particular morning the conversation had turned to the topic of dwindling vocations and about half way through the conversation the young priest suggested that maybe we as brothers should consider 'going all the way', that is, not stop at being just a brother but 'up our game and go for the real deal' and become priests! Being young and a little feisty I remember I winced with indignation. I noticed, to my amazement, that none of the other brethren appeared to be even remotely perturbed by Father's musings. Father continued by pointing out that if it was a lack of academic aptitude on our part then there were specially adapted courses available for men in our position. To this day I do not understand how I restrained myself. I do not know what bothered me most, the curate's comments or the apparent indifference of my confreres to what he was saying. When he left a number of the brothers laughed and spoke of how much they enjoyed my growing discomfort as the young cleric had offered his advice. Very quickly the brothers explained why they took it all on the chin, pointing out that the priest was young, would quickly learn and that his attitude was in fact very prevalent. I remember that around that table there were men with several degrees, including doctorates. There were authors and brothers who had served in management for years. I guess what I had not really budgeted for was the humility and prudence of the brethren. I must confess that while all of us, including the curate, have all travelled a long road since that day it crass ignorance regarding the vocation of the religious brother still irks me. This is particularly offensive when found in clergy. In my experience, few grasp the unique beauty of the call to be a brother and how it can enrich the community of faith.

Career-clerics form a sub-section of the disease that is clericalism. Some priests have a healthy attitude to being in a position of responsibility and are able to root it in service and a genuine desire to make a difference. This healthy and appropriate way of responding to stewardship will always be rooted in prayer and is usually marked by a prophetic zeal for the gospel. In my view any priest who has not clearly demonstrated a track record of compassion for people, especially those caught in the mess that can be life, should not be a local leader and certainly not a bishop. I acknowledge that the person in authority needs a certain toughness as well as compassion, to be able to face what may land on his desk. I am aware of a number of instances when a bishop has been unable to deal with an individual priest who has been found to be living in a way that is incongruent with his priesthood. I mean no judgement in this regard and I am not speaking the language of censure. I am sorry that a bishop as spiritual father should be unable to address the situation. The issues involved can vary, but will often be related to lifestyle and will sometimes be relational. The inability to deal with issues often can be on both sides: a particularly recalcitrant priest who has little or no understanding of obedience; a bishop who has no stomach for hard decisions, who wishes to remain popular, who has a log in his own eye or who simply feels that as he is near seventy, these issues are better left to his successor. These standpoints might be understandable and human, but they prove disastrous for reform and renewal in the church.

The enemy at the table

In discussing the present difficulties of the Irish church it is surely legitimate to ask is there an actual root cause of the problems. If so, can we name it? The answer to this question is complex. The easiest thing in the world is to develop a persecution complex and to see threat every-where. There is certainly much hostility and it is true some people have an anti-church agenda, though this is often born of hurt. We are often angry with the media, accusing them of being godless and militantly secular, and fail to see in ourselves the very thing we berate in them – the fact that we indulge in blanket condemnation. Despite some unfairness, there are people in the Irish media who remain highly professional and have retained an inter-est in church and faith matters. I believe there are other enemies within the Irish church that we might be less comfortable facing.

In general what I am speaking of here is the dis-func-tionality, or perhaps counter-witness, of an unhappy priest. Unhappiness is not a crime. One should not be blamed or judged for being unhappy. Unhappiness is a state and is not a very healthy place to be. Unhappiness disempowers us. Unhappiness drains us, saps the lifeblood out of us. It is possible that we are unhappy and we struggle to name it. Priests and religious do not have a monopoly on unhappiness. There are plenty of single, married, widowed and separated people who struggle with unhappiness. However, the unhappy priest or religious has an added dimension with which to struggle. They are publicly professed ambassadors of the good news and with this comes great expectations and burdens. Before developing this point any further let me clarify what I mean here by unhappiness. I am not referring to the blues. This is not in the realm of not liking Mondays. Nor indeed are we speaking of clinical depression, which needs medical intervention and supervision. This is something ingrained. It is like a default position.

Sometimes it is characterised by cynicism, which is a well-known foe of the spirit, sometimes simply an absence of joy. I have been amazed looking at the faces of a group of priests (or occasionally religious) and seeing how lifeless or joyless then can look. They can be tired and overworked, and many of them are no longer young, but they are ministering and should be witnessing to the Paschal Mystery which culminates in Easter joy. Why is it that sometimes clergy and laypeople alike confuse being holy with being sombre or, worse still, sad? The unhappy priest is usually aged between thirty and ninety. He has given up on reading, except maybe the newspaper. He has certainly not studied anything for a long time, except maybe the horses. He has no spiritual director. His friends, if he has any, are all priests. He is afraid of silence. He would never go on a directed retreat. If he goes at all, it is on a diocesan retreat where he prays a little but mostly enjoys the craic and seeing old buddies whom he has not seen since last year. His sense of humour, if not completely gone, can be hard to find. Sometimes he does not know who he is sexually, or even more generally who he is emotionally or psychologically. He is often someone who has done no work on himself. By this I mean that he has never engaged in psychotherapy or even a little one to one counselling. Even though he may have several academic qualifications and be a skilful orator, he has the emotional intelligence of a newt. He will often give himself away when asked how he is, or how he is feeling, as he will launch into a summary of how busy he is or of all that's going on in the parish. The unhappy priest is sad indeed. If his inner world remains unattended, he can move to being a danger to himself and others. Addictive and fixated behaviour can ensue. Needless to say this all becomes an explosive cocktail if he is ministering to the broken and vulnerable as he often is.

Please note there is no judgement intended or even inferred here. Surely if our pastor, priest or religious is living in long-term unhappiness it is neither healthy nor Christian to shrug our shoulders and say it is not my problem. Surely we can develop a strategy of response, an intervention out of love. It even helps to say, 'We notice, we care, there is help and we will walk with you'. We as priests are called to prayerful solitude but if this slips into gnawing loneliness we die, sometimes years before we are buried. This is wrong in any community but in a Christian community it is anathema, or should be.

I should clarify my use of the word enemy. Without clarification it is unintentionally harsh to use it in reference to an unhappy priest. The dis-functionality of diocesan priesthood is not wilful, but it is corrosive. An unhappy priesthood is a counter-witness. It suggests that something is amiss. It bespeaks a lack of wholeness. For many this lack of wholeness is often symptomatic of a divided heart. To be half-hearted, or to nurse a divided heart, is not a happy condition. Jesus should be the desire of one's heart, the focus, the raison d'être. This is not always the case. So the unhappy priest, living in either an emotional desert or a state of emotional schizophrenia, attempts to love Jesus but is in love with another. This can end in a cul de sac; it is not a road to peace. In this sense the priest can be an enemy of himself and in his ministry be either a block or at least a cause of his community treading water. Certainly as a minister he is not operating on full power.

There is another enemy within the Irish church that we need to name. It is a group I call the doctrinal police. I can see them now coming over the hill. They are steeped in the law. They worry about rubric. They quote the law. They hearken to the past. Sometimes there are cufflinks, usually incense (I love incense myself!) and often a deep Roman collar. They profess themselves Roman, though in my experience they are often roaming. Unyielding, they remind me of the tree that does not bend but breaks. They are harsh and often have not got an ounce of compassion between five of them! I often think Jesus himself might dive for cover before their advance. Parody? Exaggeration? Perhaps. Let me be more circumspect. In the present vacuum, between the dying Irish church and the possible emergence of some new faith community centred on Jesus, a certain cry as gone up. It is essentially a fundamentalist cry. This retreat to the safety of the rule is both predictable and understandable. However, this desire for the definite and a move to the order of past days brings at best only temporary respite at a high price. In effect, it brings about more acrimony and division than it's worth. This group rather unfairly hijack the Pope Emeritus, Benedict XVI, to support their aspirations and often pit him against the present pontiff. It is quite amazing to see prominent Catholics publicly doubt Pope Francis as chosen by the Holy Spirit. They cite factions or movements in the conclave that elected him, conveniently forgetting that from the earliest days in the church there was always ambition and intrigue. They seem to doubt the power of the Holy Spirit to manage and mould all that. Apart from having

wobbly faith in God's Holy Spirit they also fall foul of the
great sin of pride. They know better than the successor
of Peter. He is in error and should repent. They fail to see
their own arrogance.

Even if well intentioned, they are doing extraordinary
damage to the church. They tend to mobilise like a mob
and will often be characterised by harsh judgement. In my
view one of the worst aspects of the doctrinal police is
their interference in priestly formation. This is the way
it works. A young, or not so young, man enters the seminary, often after having been nourished by a particular
prayer group. The group nurtured and sustained the now
seminarian and it was appropriate that they carried him
in prayer. However, at the point of beginning his formation, the challenge for the individual is to be open to
being formed, through God's grace. This is not easy, but
essential. The prayer group needs to respect the formation
personnel and programme. But here the doctrinal police
move in. The tack they take is this: the formation programme is no good. Those priests do not know what they
are talking about. A young seminarian who had come in
straight from school said to me after a year in the seminary, 'I'm out of here. I have been here nearly a year and
I have not seen Holy Mass celebrated properly even once.'
This was breathtakingly arrogant on the part of the seminarian, who had attended Masses celebrated by the finest
of priests. But it also shows how destructive it was that

the group goaded and incited him into this position. That this undermining of the seminary formation programme should be given oxygen by a couple of our bishops is reprehensible in the extreme.

It is important to say that the caricatures of conservative or liberal priests are very unhelpful and quite divisive, as well as being inaccurate. Surely the church is big enough to accommodate those who retain a love for the Latin Mass, those whose vocation has been nourished in Medjugorje as well as those who found their way through lectio divina with Merton and Nouen. Say two new priests arrive: one is very clerical, complete with collar and cuff-links; the other is a bit more hip, with jeans and Taizé cross around his neck. Which of these is a real priest? Which should we welcome? The answer is both, of course. Surely the more important questions regarding both are: is this a man of prayer? Is he passionate about Jesus and the gospel? Is he compassionate towards people? We have spent far too much energy in the pursuit of peripherals when we should be united in love and service of one another. One of the great casualties of this squandering of missionary zeal is a loss of the ability to communicate.

Lost for words
I smiled recently at a little girl who innocently referred to incense as holy smoke. I was less inclined to smile at the teacher who struggled for words to describe the sacred

host and stuttered from the word 'wafer' to the phrase 'the white thing you hold up at Mass'. Recently, giving out holy communion at a funeral down the country, in a line of about thirty people four or five responded with 'Amen', while the remainder proffered variations on 'cheers', 'nice one', 'thanks', and 'sound job'. The retired priest beside me who had a similar experience in his line said to me afterwards how offensive it was. After some discussion, though, he readily agreed with me that there was no malice intended in any of this. Rather it was an example of ignorance in the best sense of the word. The people simply did not know. They knew they were receiving something special, or at least significant and they offered thanks in the way they would on being presented with a pint of beer. In fact it is becoming more common to see people who seem not to know that they need to put the sacred host in their mouth. Some walk away with it, others make to place it in their pocket. For at least twenty years we have been having conversations about what to do about the sacramental conveyor belt that trundles on year after year. The problem is that as the conversations continue people have moved further and further from the church. We now have actually lost not one but two generations. When I started teaching first we used to say that we could rely on the grannies to pass on the faith. The reality now is that there are many grannies who have little or no interest in church.

No matter what form of prayer we lead, whether rosary, Stations of the Cross, even sometimes just a talk in church, people will say, 'Thanks for the lovely Mass'. On my return from a holiday last year a lady told me that the Parish Sister had said a few great Masses when I was away. We have not simply lost basic terminology, we have completely lost our sense of the sacred. Many of our churches are becoming increasingly noisy. Some people arrive in church chewing gum with their bottle of water or Red Bull to be entertained, happy to nip in and out for a smoke. I recently heard a small boy plead with his Dad, 'Dad please stop talking in church!'

It would appear that we are increasingly failing to engage people. Recently, in conversation with a group of young people it was obvious that they retained a residual respect for church. However if we scraped a pass on the respect test we failed to make it on the relevance factor. Is there serious communication failure in the church? How much of this is about actual language? Many of us still insist on reading somebody else's homily, or homily notes, to our longsuffering congregation. We still operate within the realm of stories, parables and catechesis while so many in the pews are into sound bites. With Facebook, WhatsApp, Instagram and so on people have become more immediate. All this is before we enter the realm of being clear about what exactly we want to communicate. It was interesting to see recently how negatively some parishioners reacted to the guidelines issued by the church on cremation. They described feeling chastised for something done, or patronised regarding their intentions. On more challenging topics many people who should know better are unclear about core matters of faith, including transubstantiation, epiclesis, as well as aspects of eschatology, including the communion of saints. We tend to be a little scattered and disunited with regard to what we preach. Do we preach the servant king? Do we preach a suffering messiah? Do we preach God as mercy? Does what we preach strike the listener as Good News? Have we fire in our belly for the message of Jesus?

Internal bleeding

Are we in the Irish church presently living and believing in Jesus? One of the core characteristics of those who are living in Christ is how they treat others, most especially those who are poor or vulnerable. This brings me to another aspect of the malaise, or inner rust, that is gradually eating away at the church. I see it as a form of internal bleeding. Strange as it may seem, the church does not always do forgiveness and healing well. I say strange because of course these things form the very raison d'être of church. We should not be surprised, then, that when we get forgiveness and healing wrong it strikes at our very core. It hurts individuals, families, communities and the church itself. When people become estranged from the church, often through the actions of the church, this constitutes haemorrhaging. This is the internal bleed that weakens us because it exposes a consistent failure on our part to be Christ-like. It stands out for me as one of the most glaring examples of how we let ourselves down as a faith community.

I am sure many of us know people who can say that the church has hurt them. This in itself is a bit of a euphemism, because they were actually hurt by an individual, even if the individual may have been acting on behalf of the church or occupying a role in the church. We all know people who, often through no fault of their own, find themselves outside in the cold looking in on a church that they love.

Marita is someone in this situation. When she was twenty-four, Marita married Tim. It was a church wedding. They seemed made for one another. Both the couple and their families rejoiced in their love Three months into their marriage Marita discovered that Tim was having an affair with a girl at work. She was broken-hearted but forgave him. Soon after it happened again with another girl. Again, with great difficulty, Marita forgave Tim. A month later, same again. They decided to begin a new life together in Australia. Two months after they left, Marita was home alone and totally broken. The reality was that Marita had married a serial adulterer. What did the church say to her?

Aaron is one of the loveliest people I know. He is thirty.

He is bright and funny and handsome. He also has a deep love of God and a real vibrant spirituality. I thought at one time that he might be interested in the priesthood. That is, I thought so until he recently told me of his dream, his heart's desire. Aaron hopes to meet another man who will love him and whom he will love for the rest of their days. What does the church say to him?

I have asked two questions which should not label me as liberal or as a renegade. Nor should I be seen as soft or weak on church teaching. I believe and I preach the beautiful message of the gospel founded on the solid tradition of the church: our sexuality is a wonderful gift from God. I preach the sanctity of marriage. However, mindful of Jesus in his clear presentation of the ideal and his repeated compassion for those who find themselves in the mess of life, I must ask these questions. It is imperative that we find ways to lead, nudge, encourage, convince and stop the finger wagging and tut-tutting. One of the tell-tale signs that we are well into the church's death throes is that many people have stopped fighting with us, especially when we resort to pointing the finger and booming 'thou shalt not!' In the face of our pious priggishness many simply yawn and walk away. Surely we can do better than this for Jesus, if for no other reason. Jesus is more attractive and exciting than this.

Mindful of the attractiveness of Jesus my thoughts turn to those who at one time thought they had a religious vocation, or perhaps feel that they still do. In this small little island of ours there are many thousands of women and men who spent short or long periods within religious life or the priesthood. Many will have tried it out for a while, discovered it was not for them, left and hopefully were the better for their experience. Sadly, this is not true for so many. The reality is that there are many who had a less than happy experience. Sometimes this negative experience was the time spent within the religious order or seminary, but it is often about the manner of their departure. Many were very badly bruised by their experience. When the system of formation helped people realise that the way of life was not for them, helped them leave and re-integrate into lay life, then this of course was a good thing. What about those who remain badly-scarred? What of those who were sent home for the most trivial of reasons? What of those who were told to go, who went in the dead of night, who cried the night before they went home and many nights since? I have met old men who were dismissed many years ago and remain a priest or brother at heart. I believe there are many women and men out there who were harshly treated by the system. They received a cold cruel dismissal. We did not always have a bishop or provincial who were prepared to go the extra mile. Thankfully today we have a few of those. I understand that not everybody is suitable for religious life or priesthood, but is formation not at least partly about finding that out?

When it does not work out, surely we can find words of thanks, of blessing for the future, never mind aftercare or pastoral follow-up. Sadly we have not been slow to use the language of failure and censure. The bleed is not confined to those who left during formation. There are droves of former religious and clergy, many admittedly who are happy and fulfilled as married or single people. But there are also those who are still very hurt and battered by their experience of a church that they once embraced as their dream, their life. Perhaps some of them should be invited back, even as collaborators or associates. Don't all of them deserve to hear us say that we are sorry, that we could have cherished them better and that we did not mean to be cold or dismissive?

I knew a bishop once who was brilliant. He was funny and intelligent and kind. He was a great communicator. He was also human, he made mistakes, and I think he was lonely. He lost his way a bit. His brokenness and fragility became the curiosity of the nation. In a way there is no surprise in that. In my imagination I had this idea that when the day came and he was like a rabbit caught in the highlights, frozen in fear, that maybe a few of his fellow bishops might show up and stand beside him, but that did not happen. I think there were one or two who contacted him, Nicodemus-like, under cover of darkness. The broken bishop was not only frozen in fear, he was alone. His fellow shepherds failed their brother in his hour of need. What amazes me is that the leadership of the church repeatedly fail to have the moral courage and gospel wisdom to implement the old distinction between the sin and the sinner. Is it beyond our capability to stand in the market square and acknowledge that, though this man has made some serious mistakes that we do not condone, he is our brother? Can we not say that while we are mindful of those who may have been hurt by these mistakes we will not condemn him? Would this not be prophetic leadership? Would this not be an attempt to model the gospel? Thankfully this man remains a true inspiration. His experience of the cross and the graces he has received from shouldering it have rendered him rich indeed, richer than some who remained cosy on the episcopal cushion. Sadly, even the most faithful daughters and sons of the church have learned that once they mess up they will feel the winds of isolation begin to blow in around them. The institution protects the institution but not the individual. I remember another bishop who strayed from the path and paid publicly. In his case, even in his old age and after a lengthy period of trying to atone, we could not find it within us to give him a gracious, even muted welcome. Sometimes our shepherds fail us, and sometimes we fail our shepherds.

Evil spirit

Our tendency has been to sacrifice the individual for the sake of the universal. This means we fail to recognise that the true measure of us as a group lies in how we treat our most vulnerable member. This is true of novice, seminarian or bishop. The reality is that even within all that is beautiful in the church, there is the tendency to abuse power. Where does this tendency come from? Plenty would say that this and many of the ills outlined above come from the evil spirit. Perhaps as we come towards the end of a chapter that has been very much immersed in the death of the church in Ireland it is timely to ask ,'What of the devil in all this?'

Except for while reading the *The Screwtape Letters* by C.S. Lewis (the brilliant fictional letters from a senior Demon, Screwtape, to his nephew, Wormwood, a Junior Tempter) I have never been much drawn to the devil, at least not to the pointed-tailed, fork-brandishing, horned creature. Yet I find it fascinating that if prompted by the gospel to mention the devil in a homily it always evokes something bordering on delight in a few of the regulars. This almost gleeful response to even a cursory mention of Satan reminds me of two rather dangerous positions in our church today. They are both extremes. The first of these is the group of people who are conscious that the devil is everywhere, that he is always about to jump out on them. He may even be in the porridge. These can be a joyless, jittery lot and who would blame them? They live on a battlefield. The other extreme is the group who tell you there is no such thing as the devil and certainly there is no hell. They promote the idea that the devil was more or less dreamt up to keep us in line, and that an all-loving God would not send us to hell. This group do not like when you speak of free will as the great gift of God or when you say that it may well be our exercise of that same gift that may lead us to the loss, however temporary, of the Lord's companionship. So a very important question remains. Is there such a thing as the devil, and what is its bearing, if any, on the present death within the Irish church? I believe that anyone who becomes aware of the spirit, both within themselves and within the community, quickly recognises both the evil spirit and God's Holy Spirit. Indeed there may well be a particular argument that points out that the work of the evil spirit thrives when people feel that he does not exist. While I do not subscribe to the notion that there is no such thing as the devil I do believe we should spend more time finding out as much as we can about the Holy Spirit. Anybody who works on developing a vibrant relationship with the Spirit will quickly realise how enriched a life lived within that Spirit can be.

With such a preponderance of ecclesial rust how do we make sense of the daily dying in our church today? Could it be that we are actually living chapter fifteen of John's gospel? Is this the withering, the pruning and the burning? Is what we are experiencing less about the evil spirit, and more about the Holy Spirit? Are we experiencing the pruning? Are we to be chopped down? Or are we to be left to wither? Before we can even get near an answer to these questions we must address as honestly as we can how in fact we got here? How have we come to this?

> So little cause for carolings
> Of such ecstatic sound
> Was written on terrestrial things
> Afar or nigh around,
> That I could think there trembled through
> His happy good-night air
> Some blessed Hope, whereof he knew
> And I was unaware.
>
> – Thomas Hardy, 'The Darkling Thrush'

Every renewal of the church essentially consists in an increase of fidelity to her own calling. Undoubtedly this explains the dynamism of the movement toward unity. Christ summons the church, as she goes her pilgrim way, to that continual reformation of which she always has need, insofar as she is a human institution here on earth.

> – *Unitatis Redintegratio*, II.6

†

TWO

How Did We Lose Our Way?

When the other ten heard this they were indignant
with the two brothers, but Jesus called them to him
and said, 'You know that among the pagans the rulers
lord it over them, and their great men make their
authority felt. This must not happen among you.'

– Matthew 20:24-26

I am a sailor, you're my first mate
We signed on together, we coupled our fate
Hauled up our anchor, determined not to fail
For the hearts treasure, together we set sail.

– Johnny Duhan, 'The Voyage'

The Tuam scandal

As I write, the newspapers and the airwaves are jammed
with the horror of the Tuam mother and baby homes and
related stories from an Ireland that may well be past, but
whose legacy remains embedded in the Irish church of
today. Once again we are encountering some very ugly
aspects of the church. Whether we like it or not these

dark chapters are part of us and we share, to some degree, the responsibility for them. We certainly have a duty to ensure that these torturous dynamics are not repeated. The difficulty with a lot of this murky material is actually accessing the truth. There are several things that cloud the highly sought-after truth. Amongst these are things over which we have little influence, such as the passage of time, poor records and the lack of living witnesses.

Something else about the present discussion on the Tuam homes that is giving me food for thought is the role of the media and the concept of victim. The easiest thing in the world is to go off on an anti-media rant. This contributes very little to the discussion except more negativity, of which there is no shortage. There can be little doubt about the value of good quality investigative journalism. It has served us well both in church and state. Of course there will always be those with an agenda. Those who seek to harm the church. The church may even have harmed some of the journalists in question. When the media offers us only sound bites, neglecting the nuance and shades of the story, they sell us short. There is a tendency to concentrate on the what, when and who questions and neglect the more difficult why question. Pointing to who did what and when lends itself to neat but emotive headlines and it more readily sells the story. There is less immediacy, and less thanks in the more reasoned argument or discussion which seeks to shed light on why some of these awful things happened. Any attempt to understand the complexity involved is often seen as an attempt to make excuses. But if we do not make some attempt to understand why these things happened, then we increase the likelihood of repeating maybe not the minutiae but the broad strokes of our darkest chapters. Of course another central truth, which is unpalatable to many, is that church and state were so bound up together that both share massive responsibility.

I would suggest an interesting way to look at several of these topics – in particular mother and baby homes – might be to acknowledge the macro position of the state and the micro position of the church. Once we do this, we see a plethora of victims, from baby to mother, grandparents to nuns, and then we can ask necessary questions. Where were all the men, the fathers? A really fascinating question might attempt to tackle the notion of a unique brand of Catholicism within the Irish church, and an equally unique brand of human sexuality within Irish Society. Do such things exist? It has been suggested that just as we brought wonderful things with us as we went all over the world – music, culture, passion, and missionary zeal – so too we brought alcohol abuse and unhealthy sexuality. Recent revelations of some horrible abuse stories both in Canada and Australia have a distinctly Irish origin. I am sure that the church has a lot to answer for but I think it might suit many if we could simply leave it there and let the church carry the can for all our darkness. I wonder if it is also connected with being a little island surrounded by water? Maybe it's connected with always being kicked, plundered and invaded? Did the burden of saying nothing become too much?

Sexuality

At a time when we could be forgiven for thinking that nothing could shock us anymore, we find ourselves struggling to come to terms with another dark chapter of our past. We are brought back to an Ireland that viewed pregnant unmarried women as 'fallen'. It is a harsh and uncompromising term. Where did it come from? With the term came a whole series of implications. A 'fallen woman' was shameful, embarrassing to her family and friends. She was to be banished, hidden away and often disowned. Like so many aspects of life in the Ireland of the time this concept originated in a beautiful aspect of church teaching. Sometimes it is necessary, in all this mess and accompanying fracas, to remember the church teaching at issue. The church has continuously taught that our sexuality is a great gift from God and that it belongs within the committed loving context of marriage. By extension the church believes that it is within the context of a stable loving family that children our best served. It is quite extraordinary, given the beauty of the Christian message, that we have managed to end up 'doing sexuality so badly'.

It seems at the heart of so much of our mess is a twisted, or at least very badly misunderstood, notion of ourselves as sexual beings and how to act in the world. What is of particular concern is that the Irish Catholic brand of sexuality seems to have developed into a unique mix of fear, secrecy and sanction. It is not possible to discuss this as completely separate from the church and power, nor as disconnected with the success of the church.

It seems to me that in much of our approach to the God-given gift of sexuality there is both a lack of understanding and a lack of respect for what is actually involved in living our sexuality in a healthy way. One aspect of this is underestimating the power of the sexual force within us. Did we really believe that putting on the lid and tightening it firmly was an appropriate way of handling this pressure cooker? Did we not understand that the pressure would build and build to the point of explosion? Another aspect of the problem manifests itself in the lack of respect for sexuality as gift. How did we fail to see that unless the gift is used, or at least channelled in a wholesome way, then it sours, stagnates, poisons?

Within this conversation we must at least nod to celibacy. Many see this as a significant part of our problem. What if celibacy were done way with...? I am not convinced by this argument. I believe when celibacy is not lived healthily it will lead to unhappiness, lack of freedom and a deadening of joy. On the other hand, when celibacy is lived healthily, something I believe is not possible outside a rich prayer life, then it frees, empowers and fulfils.

Secrecy

The element of secrecy in Irish sexuality has often been dressed up as respect or prudence. In fact it has caused much harm. Of course it is necessary to have appropriate boundaries. Confidentiality is very important but this has been invoked to both bind the already powerless and vulnerable and also to protect the abusive and corrupt.

Much has been written about the damage done by secrecy but the topic is more complex than we are led to believe. This statement can be explained by a couple of contemporary examples. Take the example of the child protection guidelines on counselling in school. Going back to the pre-child protection procedures student students often sought reassurance that confidentiality was one hundred per cent set in stone, either prior to presenting in the actual counselling situation or quickly on. Now while one might argue that such a guarantee could never be given, the new procedures formally and definitively forbid such a possibility. I understand and accept why this is necessary. However, I have met a number of people over the years who cited this as a reason for delayed or non-disclosure. Another interesting corollary of the new procedures was the introduction of a pane of glass in the door of the counselling rooms. This was a measure designed to protect both the teacher/counsellor and the student/client. But in the weeks following the insertion of glass panels the number of students attending counselling dropped by a third. As one student remarked, 'I don't want half the sixth form to know I am going to counselling!' Again no one would argue against the necessity of the measure but an on-going conversation around the accessibility of the counselling is crucial. In the same vein, one would acknowledge that certain secrets exist to value one's privacy, and protect the sacred. However, the prevalence of dark secrets that shut people down, bound and paralysed, stifled and isolated people in their pain became all too common.

Power
Power is of itself a good thing. Power is potential. Power within the context of the church is best used to promote the message of Jesus in the gospel. At the end of a day or a week, it is beneficial to honestly ask oneself, how did I exercise power? How did my use of power impact people? Were they in turn empowered? Were they inspired, enthused and emboldened to be more themselves and to put their gifts at the service of the church? Or did people walk away from me shut down, shut up, disappointed and frustrated? Was their enthusiasm and creativity dampened or extinguished by my caution and lack of freedom? Perhaps one of the great abuses of power is stagnation,

fear of making a mistake. The desire to be loved or to be popular can disempower anyone in leadership.

Cosy relationship with the state

Much has been written on the De Valera–McQuaid era. I think most people would acknowledge that the Catholic Church had a special place in Ireland in terms of privilege and influence. That time has past. Some will lament this fact others rejoice in it. The reality is that such a relationship is now neither acceptable nor is it appropriate and whether it was in the past a more complex question. Today such an approach would lack cognisance and respect of our Christian, Jewish and Muslim sisters and brothers. That is not to neglect our fellow citizens who have abandoned creed or church and those who never belonged to one in the first place. It would be lovely to record here that we as a community of faith are embracing the new Ireland and the new opportunities it gives us as followers of Jesus. Sadly, it is not so much an embrace as dragging and fighting against, though it is never too late for graciousness. Hopefully there will be no return to the episcopal belt of the crozier or the summoning phone call. There might well be a shout from a shepherd out on the edge, smelling of sheep, inviting us live like Jesus. It will not be a call to subjection but to collaboration.

We will always have to be careful of the danger of snuggling up to the civil authority. While we need to recognise that civil authority will at times make legitimate and timely criticism of the church we have seen how ruthless and opportunistic our political leaders can be in this regard. This should come as no surprise given their natural consciousness of constituency. The reality is that we have paid a huge price for our success and our dalliance with those in civil power. If the death knell marks the end of this then it surely is a welcome dirge!

Prayerful priests

We all want to be loved, to belong, to feel like we make a difference, to be special to someone. Through prayer, everyone (whether a priest, religious or layperson) has had some experience of being loved. But when a priest no longer prays his ministry gradually slides into a reckless place. This is not to say that he is not a good person or to suggest that his work is not valuable. I could work well as a teacher, or social worker or good community worker, but as a priest I know that the less I pray, the less I can bring Jesus to my work. A bishop who, for whatever reason, is not steeped in prayer should resign. At the very least he should take time out of active ministry to do serious soul work, to re-immerse himself in his unique personal relationship with Christ. I say this with love and respect, but I say it very directly. The stakes are too high. Do we need clever bishops and priests? Of course we do.

Do we need priests who are good communicators? Yes we do. Do we need priests who are hard working? We sure do. But now more than ever we need holy priests. By holy I mean reflective and prayerful, giving substantial time to sacred silence.

We will have fewer and fewer priests. If nothing else, this will force the emergence of a very different type of church. Effectively, it will mean a lay-led church. I believe this to be a good thing. Sadly, we have engendered a spiritually disempowered laity. In the main they rely much too heavily on the priest. There is huge work to be done in the area of re-catechising the laity regarding their role, their power, their vocation. One of the problems is that so many people will talk excessively and needlessly in church, largely through a loss of the sense of the sacred, and yet within the actual liturgy they have lost their tongue. Voiceless, they are a loss. Is this because of dead language or empty ritual? Is it that the priest talks too much or gives off territorial vibes?

We have lost far too many priests and religious. I am not speaking of those who left happily of their own volition, but of those who were squeezed out, starved out, burnt out. I really mean the colourful, scrappy, prickly guys who just did not fit. Sometimes they were just too big of heart and spirit. Sometimes we were just that bit too small, narrow and mean-spirited to hold them. When we could not find space or a way of gently holding the late, beautiful and brilliant John O'Donoghue, it says more about us than him. A few years back, after I had publicly read O'Donoghue's 'Beannacht, For Josie', a young seminarian remarked, 'Sure, he's a pantheist!' – another box, another tick, another judgement.

While the church of tomorrow, if there be such a thing, will be most likely lay-led, there will still be a role for the priest. Hopefully this role will be focused on the breaking of the word and the breaking of the bread. We will need the priest for the celebration of the Eucharist; when the faith community has prepared well for the celebration and invites the priest to travel to be with them in this sacred action. No priest, no Eucharist. It follows from this that the community that fails to produce a single priest community may well have to wait on the celebration of the Eucharist. Many think that the solution is to bring in priests from other cultures and traditions but I am unconvinced by this argument.

> I shall be telling this with a sigh
> Somewhere ages and ages hence:
> Two roads diverged in a wood, and I–
> I took the one less travelled by,
> And that has made all the difference.
>
> – Robert Frost, 'The Road Not Taken'

Brothers, these diseases and these temptations are naturally a danger for each Christian and for every

curia, community, congregation, parish and ecclesial movement; and they can strike at the individual
and the community levels

    – Pope Francis, Presentation of the Christmas Greetings to
the Roman Curia, 22 December 2014

†

THREE

THE ATTRACTIVE ELIXIR
OF FALSE HOPE

Behold I stand at the door and knock. If anyone hears my voice and opens the door, I will come in and eat with that person, and they with me

– Revelation 3:20

Soft as the voice of an angel,
Breathing a lesson unheard,
Hope with a gentle persuasion
Whispers a comforting word:
Wait till the darkness is over,
Wait till the tempest is done,
Hope for the sunshine tomorrow,
After the darkness is gone.

– Septimus Winner, 'Whispering Hope'

Hope

Hope is one of the most neglected of the Christian virtues. Religious people are regularly accused of being joyless. Indeed sometimes religious people confuse holiness with sadness. This was my experience on a number of occasions.

Sometimes you will see this is in an individual when they pray or come into a church. Sometimes a pained or sad expression comes over them. This is perhaps an attempt to be serious or maybe an attempt at reverence. The problem with this pained posture, is not only is it unnatural and difficult to sustain, it actually puts people off. The reality is that people should be drawn to us because of how we love each other and because of the joy we exude. Christians are not meant to be sad. It is no accident that the present pope began his papacy by reminding us of the joy of the gospel. I am grateful to the Lord that I have been blessed with the great gift of hope. I begin this chapter noting the importance of hope in the life of the Christian. I also state my own belief, hope and trust in the Lord. I can also be hopeful for the church. I am hopeful for the life and continuance of the Universal Church, not least of all because Christ is present within the church.

When it comes to the Irish church I am more cautious, indeed more hesitant. Do I have any hope for the future of the Irish church? Perhaps I do have a modicum of hope. I am sure a faithful remnant will survive. I remain unconvinced that a substantial and vibrant Irish church will emerge. I think this will be shaped by what we as a church do over the next five years.

Denial

The origin of my lack of hope for the church in this country is the presence of denial throughout the church, but most especially within our leadership. There are no hooters sounding, no shrill alarm bells going off. I do not hear our leaders gearing themselves up for emergency. I believe the icebergs we have hit over the past decade are in fact minor compared to what is up ahead. We have managed to perfect a language of denial, most particularly a language of false hope. It's as if we say, 'it will be all right on the night', as a kind of mantra to one another and to ourselves. This mantra protects us from the awful reality of the truth and also gets us off the hook. It allows us to shirk our responsibility. This is the responsibility that we all share because of our baptism. This is our call to be workers for the building of God's kingdom. There seems to be very little recognition, never mind ownership, of the fact that we are in a state of emergency. This is a real crisis. There is a crisis in vocations, a crisis in religious practice, a crisis in leadership but most of all I believe there is a crisis of faith and a crisis of identity.

False hope

Before examining the need to call an ESE (Ecclesial State of Emergency), I will say a little more about the denial or false hope with which we reassure ourselves. The church of our grandparents was a place of certainty. This certainty was reinforced by the key voices of authority, most especially that of the church. People sought certainty and by and large they got it. It is natural to want evidence, to want to see proof. At the time of Jesus people wanted a sign. People still want a sign. Paradoxically, though we have never before had such a glut of information at our fingertips there has never been such doubt, such uncertainty. People continue to search but for the most part remain hungry. Here in Ireland we are well into a new paganism. The isle of saints and scholars is now a post-Christian island on the edge of Europe.

We are living in a spiritual wasteland. The evidence for this is overwhelming; there is a dearth of vocations, dwindling church attendance and the annual sacramental conveyor belt that confirms hundreds of children we are unlikely to see again. This is all against a backdrop of for the most part very quiet bishops. There is also loss of religious language, a lack of respect for the sacred and widespread ignorance of the person of Jesus. Another way of citing the crisis of faith is to acknowledge the loss of hope, the loss of meaning, the loss of the sense of belonging or sense of purpose. This is the ecclesial rust that is eating away at the church. My main contention in this chapter is that in all this, false hope has emerged. It is both an attractive, but ultimately dissatisfying elixir. I will examine three related phenomena the social consciousness of our youth, the growing allure of mindfulness and the new religious fundamentalism.

Youth as sign of hope

The annual sacramental conveyor belt for First holy communion and confirmation also fails to yield much by way of commitment to the sacramental or liturgical life of the church. I pray that some bishop may have the courage to stop the conveyor belt and announce that there will be no confirmations for the next two or three years, and that after that a confirmation preparation course would be offered in Transition Year. After completion of the course those who want to could apply to be confirmed. Instead of the hundreds we confirm annually in a spiritual vacuum, we might have twenty or thirty young adults confirmed at Pentecost in the Pro-Cathedral or their local parish. They would be making their choice freely and would be passionate about their commitment and how they could enrich the life of the church.

World Youth Day is often heralded as a sign of a vibrant church. This can be illusory. While many participants testify to some awareness of a hunger for God, others speak merely of camaraderie or even delight in the craic. There is much to be commended but it is not translated into a resurgence of participation in the life of the church or a new flush of vocations to the priesthood and religious life. Nor can it be argued that young people return to make a vibrant contribution to their parish. I often hear World Youth Day described as evidence of the goodness of young people. There has always been goodness in young people.

They have a great thirst for knowledge, a great compassion for those less well off than themselves and a wonderful drive to get things done. However, they have not revitalised the life of the church. They do not seem attracted to the church, at least not enough to want to change it. Have they given up on us? It may well be that the toxins of scandal still linger, or perhaps the young cannot stomach the church's perceived stance on women, sexuality and inclusion. Many of the young people who have participated in World Youth Day have a certain respect for the church and its work but for the most part they do not intend to dedicate their lives to the same church. Social consciousness is positive and its overlap with gospel work or building up the kingdom of God is obvious. However, we should not confuse these. It is not accurate to speak of gospel work or claim to work for God's kingdom and at the same time be either ignorant of, or hostile to, the person of Jesus. The key here is lack of focus on the person of Jesus of Nazareth.

The myth of mindfulness
The decline or rejection of organised religion has exposed people's spiritual hunger. For many, the psychotherapist's couch or some other form of counselling have replaced the confessional. There is no doubt that both of these have their place and indeed value, as does prescribed medication. People live busy lives and long for the spa break,

massage and facial. While these are good things, they cannot replace a preached or guided retreat or compare with the hard work and extraordinary benefits of Ignatian exercises. People never been taught about prayer, basic meditation or contemplation. I do not say this in a condemnatory way; I lament spiritual poverty. The church should teach people to pray. Ever seen an advertisement for prayer courses? Think on the other hand of the preponderance of mindfulness workshops, even in primary schools. Teachers say that mindfulness is wonderful for calming the children. Having been a teacher, I can appreciate the appeal! However, it would serve the children and entire community well if they learned early on of the joy we experience when are 'still in the presence of the Lord'.

So what is the problem with mindfulness? In one sense there is no problem with it. It lowers blood pressure, induces calm and acts as a good stress buster. It still pales beside an encounter in prayer with the risen Lord. Sometimes we speak of things like mindfulness because within the constraints of political correctness such a term will not offend. But it sells people short. In a way it does not go far enough. For me, at best, it might be a good starting point. It could serve as part of our preparation for something much richer. Mindfulness contains the idea of decluttering our mind, or emptying ourselves. So often this is where it stops, when in fact at this point we are ripe for the most beautiful of encounters with the Divine. Emptying and decluttering could provide us with the space to be alone with God.

The space, the silence, the empty cavern is where we invite the Lord. Or perhaps he already dwells there and is awaiting us. The tragedy of mindfulness is that it brings us to a door with great expectation and leaves us there.

Danger of restorationists

At a time of crisis in the church and within the vacuum that this creates, a 'restorationist church' has emerged as a reaction. This group is developing apace. It tends to hearken to the past, which n itself is not a problem, nor indeed is a love of incense or a penchant for the Latin Mass. However, the desire for the certainty of the past can lead to harshness. Rigidity is the tendency but it is not the answer. Restorationists become finger pointers, tut-tutting, muttering 'thou shalt not' and falling back on quoting the law. They often lack joy but still appeal to many. This group has particular difficulty with the present pope. They not only criticise the Pope but have actually been abusive and disrespectful to him. I find it amazing that people who claim to be Catholic have no difficulty being not only disloyal but openly hostile to the Successor of Peter. When we shout 'I am for Benedict, I am for John Paul, I am for Francis' do we not forget Paul's warning about saying 'I am for Apollos, I am for Paul'? Will we rip each other apart? Do we not know that we are called to unity and that the only real and perfect unity is within the life of the Trinity? I believe that the restorationist movement is a real danger to the church. Those who have placed themselves in this position very quickly end up 'policing' the rest of us. This is something that can easily degenerate into a Pharisaic-like judgement pertaining to the minutiae of rubric. In the past, when we spoke of the scandal of disunity amongst Christians we probably never thought of the possibility of serious division among Catholics. This possibility is now a growing reality. Whether this will accelerate towards schism or not remains to be seen but it has already led to the haemorrhaging of commitment to the mission of the church.

Formation

There is a direct connection between the restorationists and formation. One could be forgiven for thinking that any vocations to the priesthood and religious life are better than none. I cannot agree. I believe the real crisis is not a lack of vocations but a crisis of identity. Jesus delights in Peter's confession of faith at Caesarea Phillipi, exclaiming 'Simon bar Jonah you are a happy man!' So it is amazing that a few short verses later he is saying to Peter, 'Get behind me Satan'. Why is this? How does it come about? Peter is applauded for grasping the identity of Jesus, with wisdom from the Father, but Peter soon balks at the notion of the suffering and death of Jesus. This is too much for Peter. Yet for all that, Jesus is clear that suffering and death for our salvation are at the heart of his identity. The church needs to try to come to terms with suffering. Do those in formation realise that they will arrive as pastors into communities that have suffered greatly? How do we pastor to the suffering? Has this any bearing on how we understand our own suffering? If we have not suffered can we pastor effectively?

Often those entrusted with the sacred work of formation encounter candidates who are not open to being formed. Some of these had found their way to the seminary sponsored officially or unofficially by individuals or groups that were very restorationist in outlook. It becomes a real problem when these individuals or groups will not allow the seminarian to give his all to the formation process. The individual can find himself torn between the formation staff inviting him to engage with seminary life and the other group urging him to just endure the programme and 'get' to ordination. The end result is often a very broken and damaged individual. While we all got to seminary via different – even circuitous – routes, once we arrive we need to trust in the Lord and give our all to the formation programme. It is incumbent on all who claim to support us to pray for us and refrain from any word or behaviour that may impede this work.

It is the most natural thing in the world to try to find some hope that will see us through the swirling darkness. However, we must be careful not to be deceived or slip into self-deception. I note the presence of wolves who snap and tear within the church and express my concern regarding the temptation of restoration. Never before has religious fundamentalism so threatened the world. We must both be aware of the dangers of this type of mentality and be careful as to what we place our hope in.

Today, a sinner, and shy about it,
You asked me to drive up to church, and sit
Morose as ever, telling me to slow
On corners or at pot-holes that I know
As well as you do. What is going on
Beneath that thick grey hair? What confession
Are you preparing? Do you sin as I would?

   – Seamus Heaney, 'Boy Driving His Father to Confession'

The joy of the gospel fills the hearts and lives of all who encounter Jesus. Those who accept his offer of salvation are set free from sin, sorrow, inner emptiness and loneliness. With Christ joy is constantly born anew.

   – Pope Francis, *Evangelii Gaudium*, 1

FOUR

Five Reasons the Irish Church Deserves to Die

And when he saw a fig tree in the way, he came to it, and found nothing thereon, but leaves only, and said to it, 'Let no fruit grow on you henceforward for ever.' And presently the fig tree withered away

– Matthew 21: 19

I loved you for a long, long time
I know this love is real
It don't matter how it all went wrong
That don't change the way I feel
And I can't believe that time is
Gonna heal this wound I'm speaking of
There ain't no cure,
There ain't no cure,
There ain't no cure for love

– Leonard Cohen, 'Ain't No Cure for Love'

An unpopular topic

I have been speaking for a while now about the death of the Irish church. I am still surprised to discover that many people do not believe that this is a reality. To me this is something that has been happening for a number of years and is now gaining an unmistakable momentum. I would like to concede from the outset that it is not an attractive topic. To speak of it does not engender popularity. Archbishop Charles Browne (who served as Papal Nuncio to Ireland from 2011 to 2017) spoke of the Irish church about to go off a cliff. In this chapter I wish to discuss a number of reasons why I believe the Irish church must die.

The legacy of preaching fear not love

I am amazed by how good we are at preaching a message of fear, even though the whole joy of the gospel is a message of liberating love. We did this so well. We did it with aplomb, in Dolby stereo and glorious technicolor. It became a key part of our brand. Hellfire, brimstone and damnation became synonymous with the Irish priest, part of our narrative. For a long time I, like many, thought that a lot of this either did not happen at all or that, if it did, it was exaggerated. I now have no doubt that the fear instilled by the church was real; it was effective and it bound people. I guess nothing binds or traps you like fear. This is still a reality for a lot of people. It is sad to meet people in sacrament of reconciliation who are still bound by the chains of fear, who have lived really good lives, more often than not exhibiting solid evidence of heroic virtue, wrestling in their twilight years with guilt and living in the shadow of a God who seeks rather to catch them out than set them free. This is a legacy that we should not be proud of nor have any desire to emulate. We have often preached darkness rather than light. Even though much of the overt harshness has faded we still have not managed to find a way of preaching the gospel that is radical, liberating and uncompromisingly Christo-centric. We have failed to empower, liberate and inspire and this is why we find ourselves in the present death throes. If we continue to corrupt the message of Jesus with fear and, worse still, if we do so to bolster our own power then we deserve a radical pruning. Then, if we fail to respond to the pruning, the Holy Spirit may well be left with no choice but to wield the axe!

Dysfunctional leadership

At present we have seven dioceses awaiting the appointment of a new bishop. There are a number of Irish bishops at the moment who, as required, submitted their resignations on reaching their seventy-fifth birthday and who nonetheless remain responsible for a diocese as they approach their eightieth birthday. This is madness. The delay in replacing them is damaging the church. I say this with great respect and some affection. This is not good for the bishop or the diocese. In so many ways leadership in the Irish church is tired, predictable, cosy and bland. People deserve better. Evangelisation – in an increasingly pagan Ireland – needs more.

One of the great curses of leadership in the church is the inherent lack of accountability. The bishop is quite literally 'the monarch of all that he surveys'. To be unaccountable in our work is not good for any of us. This unaccountability is endemic in the church and we have paid the price for it.

We have a duty to look after those who step into our seminaries or religious houses of formation, not to molly coddle them, but to look after them. There is a big difference between a system that has a set of taboos, a system that seeks to repress, catch out and then discard and a system that welcomes, accepts, challenges and respects. The person discerning his or her vocation in life should not meet rejection and be left to deal, alone, with an emotional mess. On the contrary, the person who discerns, or is helped to discern, that they do not appear to have a vocation to priesthood or religious life must be affirmed and nourished in their vocation through baptism to follow Christ and to contribute to the life of the church. Formation work is now more than ever among the most challenging roles in ministry.

I have encountered breath-taking arrogance in bishops with regard to formation. In some instances, seminary staff has said clearly that a particular individual should not be ordained, at least for the present. But the bishop appears to know better and goes ahead with the ordination. I could understand if this were because the bishop wanted to show graciousness, or a willingness to go the extra mile. However, other factors often seem to clinch it. It is natural that a bishop should want to ordain priests; they are the lifeblood of the Eucharist in his diocese. No priest, no Eucharist, as I have already said. Sometimes a bishop will be influenced by closeness to the ordinands family or his local parish clergy. Bishops in particular need to be really careful not to be proud.

I can hear the cries that the church is not a democracy and we must not look at it through the lens of secular governance, and this is true. The church is a community of faith, a living witness to God's abiding love for us all. We, in the church, are called to be heralds of love. In Ireland we are beginning the rocky road away from a Catholic country for a Catholic people. Thanks be to God. Alleluia! Alleluia! I would love to congratulate Ireland for doing the right thing, but sadly we are doing it because we have no choice. One of the reasons that our church leadership is in fact dysfunctional is that it attempts to lead from the top or the centre, when in fact church leadership will be most effective when it positions itself at the edge, as Pope Francis encourages us all to do. The leadership that speaks of a particular love for the poor and yet does so from a comfortable middle class position will gradually sound hollow and eventually redundant.

Promotion of a soured sexuality

To promote a healthy, joyful theology of sexuality (as opposed to a narrow, negative one) is more or less beyond the Irish Catholic church at the moment. The damage done is so great that it will take quite a while for the weeds to clear and a new sowing to take place. At the moment most people have little truck with the utterings of the male celibate church and its disgusting history within the area of human sexuality, a history of abuse, secrecy, repression, fear and hypocrisy. To say that we damaged our credibility is an understatement. The authority of the Irish church to teach about morality and sexuality is at an all-time low. We have placed ourselves on the ropes. Even in this we tend to blame others, usually the media, grumbling that they have an agenda. Of course the media has an agenda. Guess what, so do we. Hopefully ours is the gospel.

Very few people understand the Catholic Church's view of human sexuality as rooted in Jesus and moulded and fashioned through the teaching of the church. Even the phrase, the teaching authority of the church, grates on many. This is understandable. For so long we spoke from an established and unchallenged position, particularly in the Irish context. So it is difficult for us not to slip into that old stance today, even with regard to something as basic as language. If we use the old language it will, by and large, fall on deaf ears and perhaps it is good and wholesome that it does. Perhaps in no other area have we made such a mess as we have done in the area of sexual morality. Getting back our voice in this regard is unlikely and it is a voice we should be cautious in trying to reclaim. Perhaps, if we are repentant and humble enough the Lord might give us a new voice. If the Lord is in it, it will not terrify people or bind them up. If the Lord is in it, our voice can free and empower people to see and live the extraordinary gift of sexuality in a way that honours it and honours the Lord.

Indifference to the sacraments

Most people will agree that more and more people in this country are becoming increasingly un-churched. That is to say, fewer people regularly attend church. I am referring to baptised Catholics. In recent years, there has been a major shift away from the institution of the church. Recently, an undertaker told me that he sees more and more people who opt to go straight to the burial or cremation, sometimes with a humanist service and sometimes with no service at all but perhaps a poem or song. Those of us who believe that Catholic burial rites are among the most beautiful in the world need to start asking questions. Why is this happening? How much of it is our responsibility? It would be wrong to land all the blame on the church. However, to what degree does the way we conduct a funeral service fit into our overall practice in liturgy. Some liturgies are obviously well-prepared and provide a good experience for those present.

So what is good liturgy? When we come away from liturgy we should be conscious that we have been in the presence of God. This will lead to a change in us. This change is likely to be small and gradual. The change is also likely to be evident in how we treat each other. This is the Eucharist working in and through us. Good liturgy should assist us in our conversion and provide us with soul food. This is the work of the Lord and it is good for us to remember that. The work of the Lord can still be enhanced or hindered. Sacred music (and there is no real excuse for using any other type given the plethora of choice available) can really help us to pray well. Very often there is not a thing wrong with the sound system except that the person using it does not know how and does not seek assistance. Lay involvement in liturgy is good but it tends to be on 'Father's' terms. Priests often see greater involvement of the people of the parish as a threat to our own security or our narrow parochialism. We are afraid of losing power. A wedding photographer once told me that a priest greeted him on the bottom step of the sanctuary with a wagging finger and the admonishment, 'do not cross that line, this is my patch.' Wedding photographers can be intrusive and lack awareness regarding of the sacred nature of the space. But could it not be possible for us to help those working at church weddings to marry their professional task with knowledge of what is sacred?

In this discussion of why the present Irish church must die, I must touch on the increasingly unseemly sacramental conveyor belt of first holy communion and confirmation. The weeks leading up to the actual day of first holy communion and the sacrament of confirmation are usually marked with intense preparation. This hard work is evident in how well the children are drilled for the ceremony. This should not be taken for granted, given the wide range of teachers working in Catholic primary schools. We should not be surprised that there are many primary teachers who have no faith themselves. Some of these are professional and conscientious enough to do their best to deliver the sacramental curriculum not withstanding their own lack of faith. There are of course those teachers who have told me that they drag their feet on RE. They acknowledge that their lack of belief can easily become lack of interest, which the children pick up on. These teachers are careful about their unbelief, mindful that they are teaching in a catholic school. It is difficult to describe my joy when I meet a good Catholic teacher. I have met a few passionate, committed and creative Catholic teachers. I am not surprised the children love being taught by them, for they would inspire anybody.

Sometimes, even when the children are well-prepared, you can still see the desert of paganism. The children might know the rubric or protocol but will show by their behaviour they have no notion of what they have received. I am not referring to an understanding of the real presence but just a basic sense that there is something sacred or at least special. This lack of understanding is evidenced by the discarded hosts on the ground after the ceremony and by the children who go back to their seat and stick out their tongues, teasing each other regarding how long it takes to melt. After the big day itself there is little evidence of any follow-up. A small percentage of children are brought to Sunday Eucharist by their parents and most of these for just a little while. The family Mass has the potential to be a meaningful and real experience of the Eucharist. Many good things are happening in this regard but we have to be careful not to try to be entertainment just to keep children interested enough to get them through the Mass. I have been privileged to witness some excellent catechesis and evangelisation within the context of a very well prepared family Mass. This excellent work is sometimes without genuine support and nourishment within the home, which greatly reduces its benefits.

I have come to the conclusion that we should not be giving holy communion to children so young. Perhaps it could mark the end of childhood at the end of Primary school. Confirmation, as I have said elsewhere, should form part of transition year. I would much rather have a small group of young adults who freely choose to be confirmed and make a tangible commitment to be part of the life of the church. This would be much healthier than the present ramshackle, catch-all conveyor belt. It is disrespectful to the sacraments and the few who want to take them seriously. Why do we keep doing this? Why can we not let go? Is it about power and control? So many local clergy agree that we must stop doing this, but we do not. It's just too big, too widespread to be dealt with at parish level or diocesan level. If a parish or diocese were to attempt such a radical reform, many people would go to the neighbouring parish or diocese. Why have we not got the courage to let them go? We have created the monster of the 'big day'. Perhaps the disrespect is not wilful but there is a great consciousness of rights, of entitlement without any sense of responsibility: 'Sure, she is entitled to her big day, Father'. At what price? At what cost to the sacred, at what cost to the sacrament?

I have discovered recently just how much first holy communion day has become about money. One little girl received six hundred and twenty euro on her 'big day'. A lady told me recently she had taken out a large loan for her child's first holy communion and would be paying it off for quite a while. It is important to set the cost of the day in its proper context. The most important part of the day costs nothing, not one cent. This most beautiful event, the child receiving Jesus for the first time, involves no expense. And yet, in response to pressure, parents incur huge expenses. A courageous response to these abuses looks unlikely to happen at local level. The answer is clearly the remit of the Irish Episcopal Conference. Again the lack of action in this regard must be questioned because the problem is certainly not a new one.

Abuse of power

Insofar as the Irish church remains abusive it certainly deserves to die. This brings me to the fifth and perhaps most serious of the reasons why the Irish church deserves to die. Perhaps a clarification on this is timely. I take no joy in putting forward this treatise and I mean it in a very specific way. We are the vine. We should be concerned with the fruit we bear, or fail to bear. We are the salt. Have we lost or are we losing our saltiness? We are the fig tree. But are we withering? Or is this the pruning?

It is a reasonable expectation on the part of people that the bishop be holy, by which I mean, steeped in prayer. One wonders about the criteria for the appointment of a bishop. It would seem academic achievement is a priority. My own hobbyhorse with regard to leadership in the Irish church relates to the prophetic kick, the colour, the bite, the roar. This is about the roar we do not hear. Imagine if we saw a bishop standing silently – witnessing – and praying in solidarity as a family was being evicted. What about a bishop giving half the property in the diocese to the homeless or speaking up on the right to water? How many bishops have visited one of the thirty-three direct provision centres? Ever seen one in there, sleeping there, trying to wash his clothes there? No? Why not? Maybe this is too much to ask? Does the church know or care that there are over three thousand five hundred asylum seekers living in direct provision?

How are we doing in terms of gender balance, in terms of appointing women to key positions? The appointment of Marie Collins to the Vatican's Commission for the Protection of Minors was life-giving and inspired a little hope. Marie, being not only a woman of integrity but also a woman of huge courage, resigned. Her action was biblical, prophetic. She walked out to the edge of the Commission, kicked the dust from her feet and said, thanks but no thanks. Why? What did she encounter? Misogyny? Clericalism? Many of the faithful have turned to the bishops' meetings in Maynooth and heard silence. Perhaps the greatest abuse of power in the Irish church is that power is not used. Perhaps the greatest sin in leadership is inertia.

The furore regarding the National Maternity Hospital and the Sisters of Charity erupted over an issue that is at once complex and deceptively simple. It was amazing to see some media outlets strive to link the story to unpaid finances due to redress. I saw at least a hint of irony in the shouts about women's rights and dignity from those who conveniently forgot the honour and dignity of the women who make up the beautiful group called the Sisters of Charity. I hope that the sisters were not relying on the bishops to defend or support them. I am sure they had more sense. While it is understandable in some ways, the church is much too quiet. All of this is not congruent with being followers of Christ. It reinforces stagnation and darkness. This does not unbind people nor does it bring them into the light. Maybe it deserves to die.

> I do not think of you lying in the wet clay
> Of a Monaghan graveyard; I see
> You walking down a lane among the poplars
> On your way to the station, or happily
> Going to second Mass on a summer Sunday –
> You meet me and you say:
> 'Don't forget to see about the cattle –
> Among your earthiest words the angels stray.
>
> – Patrick Kavanagh, 'In Memory of My Mother'

FIVE

A FAINT GLOW IN THE ASHES?

Go, therefore, make disciples of all the nations; baptise them in the name of the Father and of the Son and of the Holy Spirit, and teach them to observe all the commands I gave you. And know that I am with you always; yes, to the end of time.

– Matthew 28:19-20

> There is treasure in our fields,
> There is treasure in our skies
> There is treasure in our dreaming from the soul to the eye
> For where- ever we gather in the light of God's grace
> And for all whom we remember, there will ever be a place
> – Catherine O'Connell, 'There is a Place'

Invitation

This is an invitation to think about how we might do things differently. It is urgent. If you understand why it is urgent, then we are already off to a good start. I am essentially inviting you to stop, pray and act. It is an invitation to be part of something bigger. It is an invitation to become part of a process dedicated to the reform and renewal of the church. Inherent in the invitation is the acknowledgement that we are in trouble. We are in trouble as a church. I believe that the death of the Irish church is likely but not inevitable. There are signs of growth – glimmers. We will see whether they are enough.

Do we have a role?

The big enemies here are denial and complacency. Sadly, some people think that no matter what happens, the church will survive. The church has indeed survived for two thousand years and will continue to do so. This is a maxim that is often repeated. However, even a cursory glance at church history teaches us that there are places and phases of growth and of dying. If we look at the history of the English and French Catholic Churches, we can see how the ecclesial landscape can be decimated at certain moments.

It is equally true that some religious orders have died while others remain. Is it possible that an order was raised up in the life of the church for a specific, time-bound mission, which once completed means the end of the particular order? Is it that the Holy Spirit, in answer to prayer, raises up an order of religious sisters to nurse and care for the aged in seventeenth century France or a group of religious brothers is founded to educate the poor in eighteenth century Spain? Is it that certain tasks can be either time-bound or place-bound or both? A particular needy group can cease to be in need of care, or might come to be cared for by the state. Within this understanding of the work of the Holy Spirit, a fascinating question emerges. Could it be that we can influence this work either in its origin or, at the very least, in the efficacy of its implementation?

Clearly if we believe in an impersonal, non-relational God – some form of vivisectionist in the sky – then none of this will make sense. In this view, God, if he is there at all, either does not care or he uses and abuses us for his own amusement. If this were the case, places and phases of ecclesial death would really be par for the course and beyond our influence. The most we could hope for would be to placate this monster God or hope not to be destroyed by his whim. Some people believe in a God like this. Naturally, they are crippled by fear. Their belief is that gloom is just around the corner. They are strangers to joy. Of course, most of those who believe in this God do not stay with him very long. Who would blame them? Very quickly, they come to believe in no God. They will announce that this life is all we have and we should live it accordingly. This does not necessarily mean a life of moral indifference or a neglect of suffering humanity. Often it is quite the opposite.

The lay-faithful have been waiting for fifty years to embrace the church of the Second Vatican Council. During this time they have experienced false start after false start, from Parish Development & Renewal to parish councils, only to see their hopes crash on the rocks of clericalism. There needs to be a revolution of the Holy Spirit. The Spirit is relying on and empowering the laity to take back responsibility for the church. I am not sure we can wait for the bishops. They seem moribund. They are too snug – not smug – but snug, cosy.

Many of today's laypeople are educated in faith matters. They are committed and passionate about Jesus. They see what is being lost. They see the spiritual impoverishment of their children and now their grandchildren. Some of these have made excellent parish pastoral workers. But they are held back. This is a shame. These are the new leaders of the church. Let's let them lead. It would appear that the Holy Spirit is teaching us that the church of tomorrow is a lay church. At least lay-led. It is a church of equality between men and women, clergy and laypeople with equal but with different roles.

Spiritual audit

Much of our current situation is incompatible with Jesus Christ. It has become increasingly difficult to even glimpse Jesus in contemporary Irish society for two reasons: the din and the pace. Our society has become very noisy and very fast. We all know the constant noise of radio, television, technology, in-store music and the frenetic pace of life. But I believe that the more serious and toxic parts of our current lifestyle are actually the inner din and the inner pace. A slow smothering of the soul, a strangulation of the spirit is well under way in Irish society. This violence is happening within us.

The easiest thing in the world is to go on a rant against consumerism or secularism, or maybe to target the media as the enemy of the church. While there may be some merit in this, it is also quite tired if not a little lazy. Such diatribes have become boring and can easily, perhaps with some justification, be dismissed as whinging or, worse, holy whinging! The ultimate antidote to this spiritual malaise lies in cultivating a deep personal relationship with Jesus. It has never before been more difficult to do this within the context of the Irish Catholic Church and the din and pace of our time.

With the din and pace of our everyday lives in mind, it might be useful for us to ask ourselves a few questions. If zero is totally trapped, stuck and paralysed with fear and ten is great freedom, where are you? If a lengthy period of silence with nothing to do fills you with dread, give yourself a zero, or close to it. When you think of death (your own, or that of a loved one) are you terrified? If so, give yourself a zero. You might dismiss these questions as contrived, or even cheesy. There is some truth in the charge. That said, they can still provide a quick check-up of our soul, like the mobile units that travel the country offering blood pressure and cholesterol checks.

Possible responses: my vision

I am hoping to form a new community dedicated to reform and renewal in the Irish church. It would have a core membership of six-eight women and men: lay, religious and cleric. This community would live and pray together. It would be a place of hospitality, with an element of parish or pastoral outreach. It would especially be a place of welcome for those hurt by the institutional church.

The core members might make a commitment of three to five years. There might be a group of more temporary members, such as a transitional deacon in his final preparation for ordination to the priesthood, someone coming up to solemn profession or maybe a student on their gap year. As well as both core and transient membership, the new community would need the wider support of an associate membership. Associate members would be crucial to the existence and development of the community. An associate member might pray, donate time or money, or simply walk in solidarity with the core and transient members. It is important that there would be many people praying for and with the community. People would be encouraged to come and pray with us.

Obviously, a community of this size would need a substantial building with appropriate living quarters for eight to ten people, a dining room, meeting room and recreational facilities. The existence or potential for an oratory, sacred space or community chapel would be essential.

Some limited facility for visitors would be desirable. There are many former religious houses that would be suitable, many of them with only minimal modification required.

I am already aware of a number of people who are interested in membership of this community. Unless this vision receives the support of a bishop or religious superior, it is unlikely to materialise. Given the nature and mission of the community, obtaining support might prove difficult.

First steps for a new community

Those who live in this new community would be characterised by simplicity, prayerfulness, gospel service and passion for Jesus. They will be imbued with a love of the church while not being blind to its ailments.

Part of the agenda for the first few years might include:

1. Developing the prayer life of the church outside the sacramental and the devotional. This would mean the actual teaching of Christ-centred contemplation, how to be comfortable with extended periods of silence and lectio divina. This would help to develop a praying church less and less reliant on the clerical. It would also help us to become more of a listening church.

2. Confronting the problems associated with the sacraments, most especially holy communion and confirmation. This would mean looking at the possibility of helping parents make a free and informed

decision as to whether or not to commit to a family contract regarding the reception of holy communion. It may well mean that confirmation would be deferred and received by much smaller numbers.

3. Acknowledging the role of the local priest in the faith community and his call to serve. Reform of the clergy and of priestly formation would be a priority.

It would be interesting to develop ways for this faith community to foster and nurture vocations. We are distracted by many things, some worthy and some more questionable, especially in our preaching. I think we do not always preach Jesus well. The truth is that Jesus of Nazareth is and remains the most pivotal figure in history. If we are to have the deep personal relationship we are called to have with him through our baptism then there is much work to do. I hope that this new community would enhance our understanding of the historical Jesus with a view to a deeper prayer life and renewed passion for the gospel.

I would like to form a group of people who would be prepared to do some work in the area of adult faith formation, using the sixteen basic documents of the Second Vatican Council and expressing what the Council taught in a fresh and accessible way.

If we can break the lethargy and find some of the creativity and freshness that comes from God's Holy Spirit, then we just might experience an awakening and postpone the wake.

> Yet stop I did: in fact I often do
> And always end much at a loss like this
> Wondering what to look for; wondering too
> When churches fall completely out of use
> What we shall turn them into if we shall keep
> A few cathedrals chronically on show
> Their parchment plate and pyx in locked cases
> And let the rest rent-free to rain and sheep.
>
> – Philip Larkin, 'Church Going'

In our times, the church after Vatican II in a renewed outpouring of the Spirit of Pentecost has come to a more lively awareness of her missionary nature and has listened again to the voice of her Lord who sends her forth into the world as 'the universal Sacrament of Salvation'. You go too. The call is a concern not only of pastors, clergy and men and women religious. The call is addressed to everyone: lay people as well are personally called by the Lord, from whom they receive a mission on behalf of the Church and the world.

> – John Paul II, *Christifideles Laici*

SIX

†

LET'S CHECK FOR VITAL SIGNS!

And all of them were weeping and wailing over her
but Yeshua said, 'Stop weeping; for she is not dead,
but she is sleeping.'

– Luke 8:52

> I the Lord of sea and sky
> I have heard my people cry
> Who will bear my light to them,
> Whom shall I send?

> Here I am Lord,
> Is it I Lord?
> I have heard you calling in the night,
> I will go Lord, if you lead me

– Daniel L. Shutte, 'Here I Am, Lord'

The current challenge

This is a very interesting, exciting and challenging time
to be a Catholic. The great richness of these days is in
our impending smallness and our deepening brokenness.
As we live church in these days we are reminded of the

centrality of the paschal mystery in the life and mission of Jesus. As followers of his, we too share this mystery. Central to this is that Jesus died that we might not die forever to our sins. Can we not argue that the world has never been more in need of the paschal mystery? More than ever the world aches for God's mercy. For this reason, I feel that we are living in a special time of grace. As we suffer, as we shrink, as we become less sure of ourselves, as we lose power and influence, Jesus comes closer and we have the opportunity for a graced moment of sacred intimacy.

Walking with Jesus and the Holy Spirit

At the last supper, Jesus shows us one of the most important journeys we can make. He walks from the table to dis-enrobe and dress as a servant. He stands from the privileged position at table, walks and then falls to his knees at the basin for washing feet. He makes the journey from cosy to crumpled. Is this part of the path for all of us? When Jesus says 'I am the way' what steps is he telling us to take? The walks of Jesus (including the walk to the temple, to Bethany, to Jerusalem, to Golgotha and to Emmaus) all present us with their own unique challenge. I wonder which of the walks of Jesus is most pertinent to us in the Irish church at this particular time in history?

I think that many of those who have left the church

or grown cold towards it might consider coming back if they saw a truly repentant church, a church that wanted to be and do things differently, a church that was more about compassion than law. I wonder; if there was a church-wide bugle call of sincere apology and invitation, would people stop and think? We would be telling people that we want to do it differently, showing that we hope to become a truly prophetic faith community and asking them, 'Will you come back and help us re-focus on the person of Jesus and become true bearers of his love, joy and peace?' With contrition and a genuine commitment to being a church of compassion what looks like dusk might prove to be dawn. How might lapsed, relapsed or collapsed Catholics respond to this? Would they consider giving us another chance?

How do we, as people of faith, respond to the present dying church? The broad answer I believe must be rooted in the Holy Spirit. It is only in the Spirit that we can have any true sense of direction in these dangerous days. The key ingredient to any response is gospel joy. It is a virtue, it comes from the Holy Spirit and it runs deep within us. It is rooted in the knowledge that we are loved totally, unconditionally, personally and passionately. It is no accident that the present Pope began his service with a reminder of the joy of the gospel. His person manifests this joy in an almost tangible way. It is this gospel joy and fidelity to the person of Jesus that characterise the faithful who have remained in the church to this day. When this current chapter of Irish church history is written, special mention will be made of these people. They are usually women, sometimes men. They have all suffered, often having experienced both abuse and loss. Again and again I am moved and inspired by their faithfulness to the Lord and I am regularly surprised by their joy. They are Christ-bearers in times of great spiritual aridity.

Conclusion

As we draw towards the end of these essays I can hear some readers ask, 'Do you think that the church in Ireland is dying or not?' The church in Ireland is dying. I see many signs of this. Is there any hope? The signs of hope are few. As I argue throughout these essays, some of what people might perceive as signs of hope are actually illusions. Lauding the strong sense of justice in the young and the huge mushroom of interest in relaxation techniques such as mindfulness are both examples of such illusions. Both these things are good in varying degrees. However, neither are evidence of an intimate knowledge of Jesus or an openness to the transformative nature of a life lived in his grace. Anything that is not rooted in the gospel, Christo-centric or enhancing the life and mission of the church is not valid evidence of vibrancy.

I hope I have not been unfair to the whole raft of devotions and those who feel nourished by them. The Clonard

Novena in honour of Our Lady of Perpetual Succour in Belfast is a really special and beautiful example of people at prayer. The novena is a time of extraordinary grace for the thousands who attend. It is led by the Redemptorists and is one of the most popular spiritual gatherings of the year. It is characterised by beautiful singing and music. Its special appeal is certainly the preaching, which is contemporary, warm and inspirational. I know quite a number of people who attend very little church activity for the rest of the year but always attend the Clonard Novena. The huge attendance at this specific event points to a broader reality – the deep hunger for soul food. This hunger runs deep and wide.

This hunger is one of the reasons I see adult faith formation as essential if the church is to survive. I think there is a real possibility to kick-start the long-awaited and desired reform and renewal of the church by constructing a creative and comprehensive programme of catechesis for adults. A preliminary six-session taster course would be a good beginning. It would demand a fresh approach to presenting the figure of Jesus in all his attractiveness, passion, radical living, teaching and his call to us. This would be best offered as a journey of discovery of the person of Jesus and of oneself. If done properly, this would significantly nourish not only individual souls but also communities, giving a much-needed focus to the ailing church.

The monasteries that have resisted decline could assist us in our awareness of the fact that we are called to have a deep personal relationship with Jesus. This is not an abstract or sentimental concept. This is serious business. It requires time, patience and hard graft. Above all it needs regular, sustained periods of sacred silence. The few remaining monasteries in Ireland have a contribution to make here. We do not need to physically go to the monastery to weave monastic strands into our lives. Once we see both the wisdom and the desirability of sacred silence – the good it does the individual soul and overall spiritual life of the faith community – we can develop the discipline to make it part of our daily lives. The time for silence in everyday life, when the external and internal noise is switched off, is not only good for mental health but it can create the sacred space for Jesus to enter. This is a new monasticism. This is kitchen monasticism.

I believe there is a real opportunity for a new form of community, such as the one I have outlined in Chapter five. It is essentially a powerhouse of prayer; it is made up of laypeople, religious and clergy; it is renowned for its welcome and it is a place for conversation about reform and renewal. It might hold possibilities for inter-faith dialogue. As the world becomes more engulfed in fear, the followers of Jesus have a clear responsibility to help take down rather than build walls. Fear leads to suspicion and fear breeds violence.

One of the most burning issues facing our ailing church is the issue of formation for priesthood. We do not need arrogant, distant, aloof and patronising priests. We have had more than a few of them. We do not need boys half choked with big collars. We do not need modern Pharisees who would try to lord over people, binding them up in rubric and law. People have suffered enough. Do we need highly qualified career clerics? Not really. What do we need? We need to form and train priests steeped in prayer, who are aware of the sacrificed involved ('Costing not less than everything'), at home with their sexuality, courageous, humorous, familiar with healthy relationships, intensely passionate about Jesus and enthusiastic about the on-going adventure with the Holy Spirit. That would be a reasonable start. The new diocesan priest will have to be something of a monk, undertaker, midwife and prophet, as well as a priest.

We are currently preparing for the World Meeting of Families, which will take place in Dublin in summer 2018. If we can keep focused on Jesus and be open to the surprise of the Holy Spirit this could be an occasion of great grace and joy.

To conclude, whether the dim light at the moment is actually twilight or dawn I am very enthusiastic about the present death in the Irish church. I am happy to keep vigil and assist in this process in any way at all, up to and including burial.

We shall not cease from exploration
And the end of all our exploring
Will be to arrive where we started
And know the place for the first time ...

Between the two waves of the sea.
Quick now, here, now, always -
A condition of complete simplicity (Costing not
less than everything)
And all shall be well and
All manner of things shall be well

– T.S. Eliot, 'Little Gidding'

I know that you face many challenges, and that the
field in which you sow is unyielding and that there
is always the temptation to give in to fear, to lick
one's wounds, to think back on bygone times, and
to devise harsh responses to fierce opposition.

– Pope Francis, Address to the Bishops of the United States,

23 September 2015

SEVEN

†

RUMBLINGS FROM THE BUNKER

What is Mass all about?

Were you ever looking for something, searching high and low, only to discover that if you stopped, dropped your head and opened your eyes you see it right there in front of you? We use phrases like 'It was under my very nose!' or 'It was staring me in the face!' We all know how easy it can be to miss the obvious. Could this also be true when it comes to the hunger for soul food or spiritual nourishment? In many areas of life – finances, health and leisure – it is often said that people are not aware of the benefits or assistance that is available to them. This may be true of us spiritually as well. Imagine a magic elixir available in Ireland could change your life. Imagine it could help everyone in every area of his or her life. Imagine it was available every day and completely free of charge. There would be some rush for it! Well it exists, but it's not magic. In fact, it's better than magic. It's called Mass.

Why is something so special and beautiful now so undervalued and underrated? Why the greatest prayer on the planet now so neglected? Mass is not only neglected, it is increasingly disrespected. Again and again I see people having a chat, putting on make-up or chewing gum during Mass. Any time I have called people out for this, they were almost indignant. I have come to the conclusion that when this happens it is not a wilful or calculated disrespect. It is a genuine not knowing what's going on, ignorance in the real sense of the word. Ignorance of the sacred is common today. I realised recently that even people who attend Mass regularly and feel they understand what is going on can be ignorant in some respects.

So why bother going to Mass?

And what exactly happens when we are there?

Fifty reasons to go to Mass

1. We gather.
2. We build community, a safe place to be with each other and with God.
3. We quieten down.
4. Blood pressure falls.
5. We pause in the madness of our lives.
6. Silence is balm for our souls, though difficult to come by.
7. We come into the church, the place built by our parents and grandparents,
8. Maintained and honoured for the sacred.
9. We remember moments of sadness and joy in our lives.

10. We say sorry to God
11. And one another.
12. We promise to try and do better.
13. We listen to God's word with our hearts as well as our heads.
14. We listen to the pastor attempt to break the Word for us, through the power of the Holy Spirit.
15. As a community we renew our faith.
16. We pray for our own needs.
17. We pray for the needs of the church
18. And the world.
19. We pray especially for the sick
20. And the poor
21. And those who have no shelter or food.
22. We present simple gifts of bread and wine.
23. We remember the last supper, as Jesus asked us.
24. We ask the Holy Spirit to change bread and wine into the body and blood of Jesus Christ present amongst us.
25. We proclaim him present in the Eucharist.
26. We give thanks for Jesus,
27. For each other,
28. For health,
29. For our gifts.
30. We pray for those who have gone to meet God before us.
31. We pray the prayer Jesus himself gave us, the Our Father.

32. Making the seven requests contained in this beautiful prayer.

33. We pray for peace,

34. We offer each other a sign of peace,

35. In this way we declare ourselves as standing against war, violence, poverty and famine.

36. We remind ourselves of our unworthiness in the presence of God and each other.

37. We bring our brokenness, our tendency to sin, to the feet of the Lord

38. And we are embraced by his compassionate love.

39. We receive Jesus present in the Eucharist, the bread that lasts forever.

40. We are changed by this experience.

41. We experience a change that is gradual but profound, taking many years.

42. We are changed to become more like Jesus, our saviour, messiah, brother and friend.

43. We are blessed.

44. And sent out to tell others about Jesus.

45. We are sent to be part of the work of Jesus,

46. To build peace,

47. To witness to hope,

48. To spread joy,

49. To be workers for his kingdom,

50. To build on the keystone of mercy!

We are involved in this sacred action, the ongoing sacred story, every time we go to Mass. What better investment could we possibly make with thirty-sixty minutes of our time?

Litany for the lost babies of Ireland
Lord,
FOR OUR ABUSE OF POWER
Forgive Us and Show Us Your Mercy
ST ITA
Pray For Us

Lord,
FOR THE HARSH WORD
Forgive Us and Show Us Your Mercy
ST MEL
Pray For Us

Lord,
FOR THE CRUEL ACT
Forgive Us and Show Us Your Mercy
ST MONINNE
Pray For Us

Lord,
FOR PUTTING A PRICE ON A BABY'S HEAD
Forgive Us and Show Us Your Mercy
ST KIERAN
Pray For Us

Lord,
FOR PUTTING OURSELVES BEFORE THE BABIES
Forgive Us and Show Us Your Mercy
ST ATTRACTA
Pray For Us

Lord,
FOR BECOMING COLD OF HEART
Forgive Us and Show Us Your Mercy
ST FINTAN
Pray For Us

Lord,
FOR TURNING A BLIND EYE
Forgive Us and Show Us Your Mercy
ST BRIGID
Pray For Us

Lord,
FOR TURNING A DEAF EAR
Forgive Us and Show Us Your Mercy
ST DECLAN
Pray For Us

Lord,
FOR FAILING TO GIVE DIGNITY TO LITTLE ONES
Forgive Us and Show Us Your Mercy
ST LELIA
Pray For Us

Lord,

FOR LACKING MORAL COURAGE
Forgive Us and Show Us Your Mercy
ST DAVNET
Pray For Us

Lord,
FOR KEEPING QUIET
Forgive Us and Show Us Your Mercy

LET US PRAY
Heavenly Father, give us a true sense of shame and remorse for the sins we have committed against your little ones. We beg for your forgiveness. Lord Jesus, you are the great healer. We ask for your healing touch for all those whose lives have been harmed by our lack of respect for little babies.

ST PATRICK
Pray For Us

OUR LADY OF KNOCK
Pray For Us

The God I don't believe in and shall never believe in[1]
the God who sneaks up on us to catch us out

the God who enjoys, or sends pain

the God who is a spoilsport, or a killjoy

the God who sends sickness

the God who wants us to live in fear

the God who is like Harry Potter waving a wand at whim

the God who wants us to always be formal with him

the God who we can only find by chance

the God who casts people into hell

the God only the intelligent can understand

the God who wants us to grovel

the God who lets us stew

the God who sees all sex as dirty

the God who ignores the poor

the God who sends AIDS as a punishment

the God who wants to ambush us

the God who can be bought

the God who is lifeless

the God who is cynical

the God who puts law before people

the God who says, 'tough luck'

the God who is regimented

the God who constantly quotes the law

the God who 'forgives' but does not forget

the God who cannot cope with our anger

the God who is owned by one church, class or culture

the God incapable of smiling at our many mistakes

the God who always demands a grade A

the God who does not want to be part of our party

the God who has a list of sins that are unforgivable

the God who prefers the rich, the powerful and the famous

the God who never cries for, or with us

the God who is not present when two men love each other

the God who is stingy and measured

the God who won't wait for us

the God who won't come looking for us in the darkness

YES, MY GOD IS THE OTHER GOD

[1]This reflection is inspired by the work of Juan Arias.

†

ACKNOWLEDGEMENTS

I wish to offer my heartfelt thanks to my family especially my brothers Larry and Tony and my sister Maria; all who form part of the faith community of St. Matthew; the 'inner Cabinet': you are my close friends who have been a key part of the journey and who continue to walk with me; Garry at Columba for his encouragement and professionalism and Alba for her patience and work in design; Joe Duffy for the warmth and empathy of his generous foreword.

Joe McDonald
September 2017

ACKNOWLEDGEMENTS